THIS COLORING BOOK
BELONGS TO:

COLOR TEST PAGE

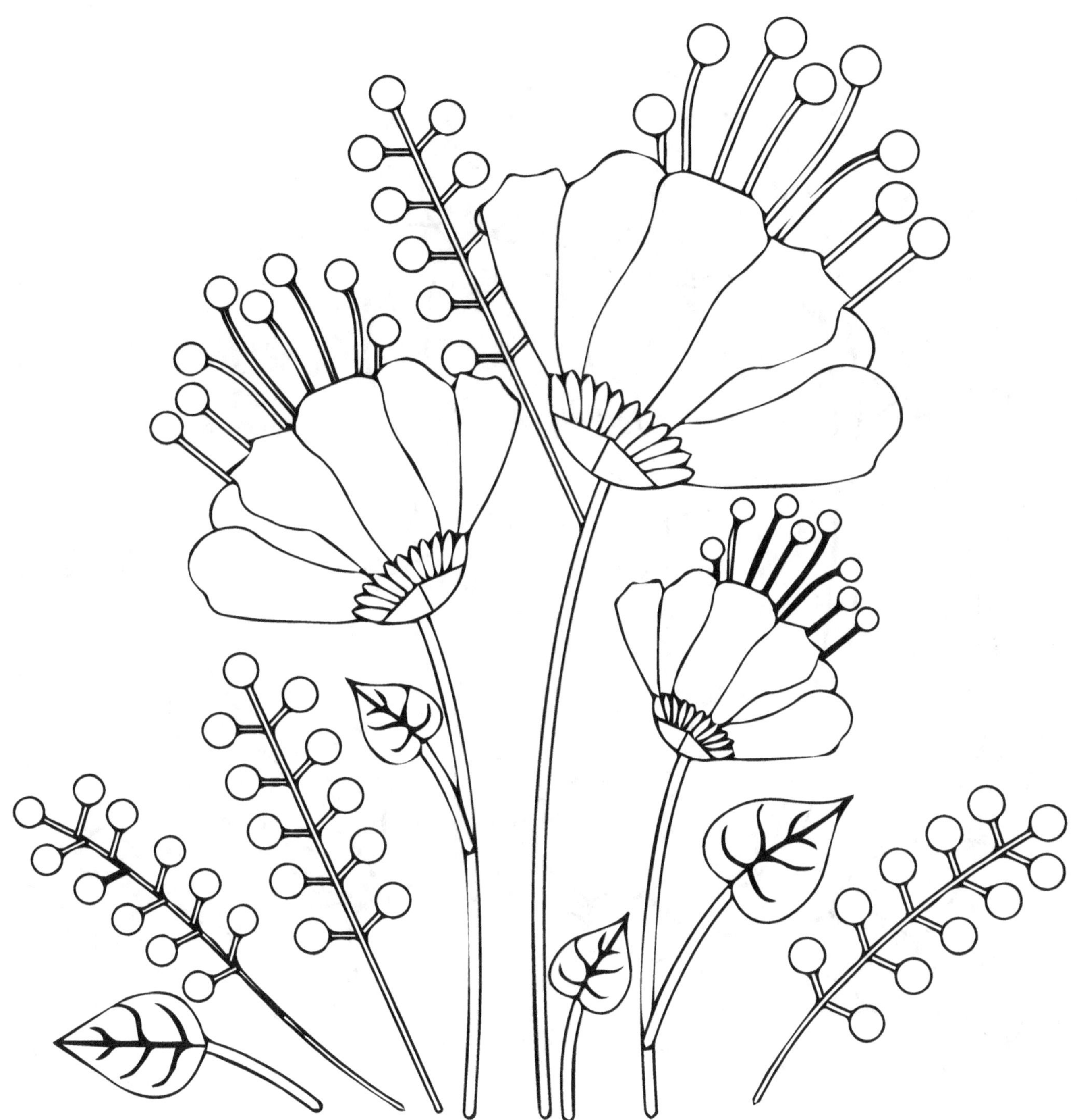

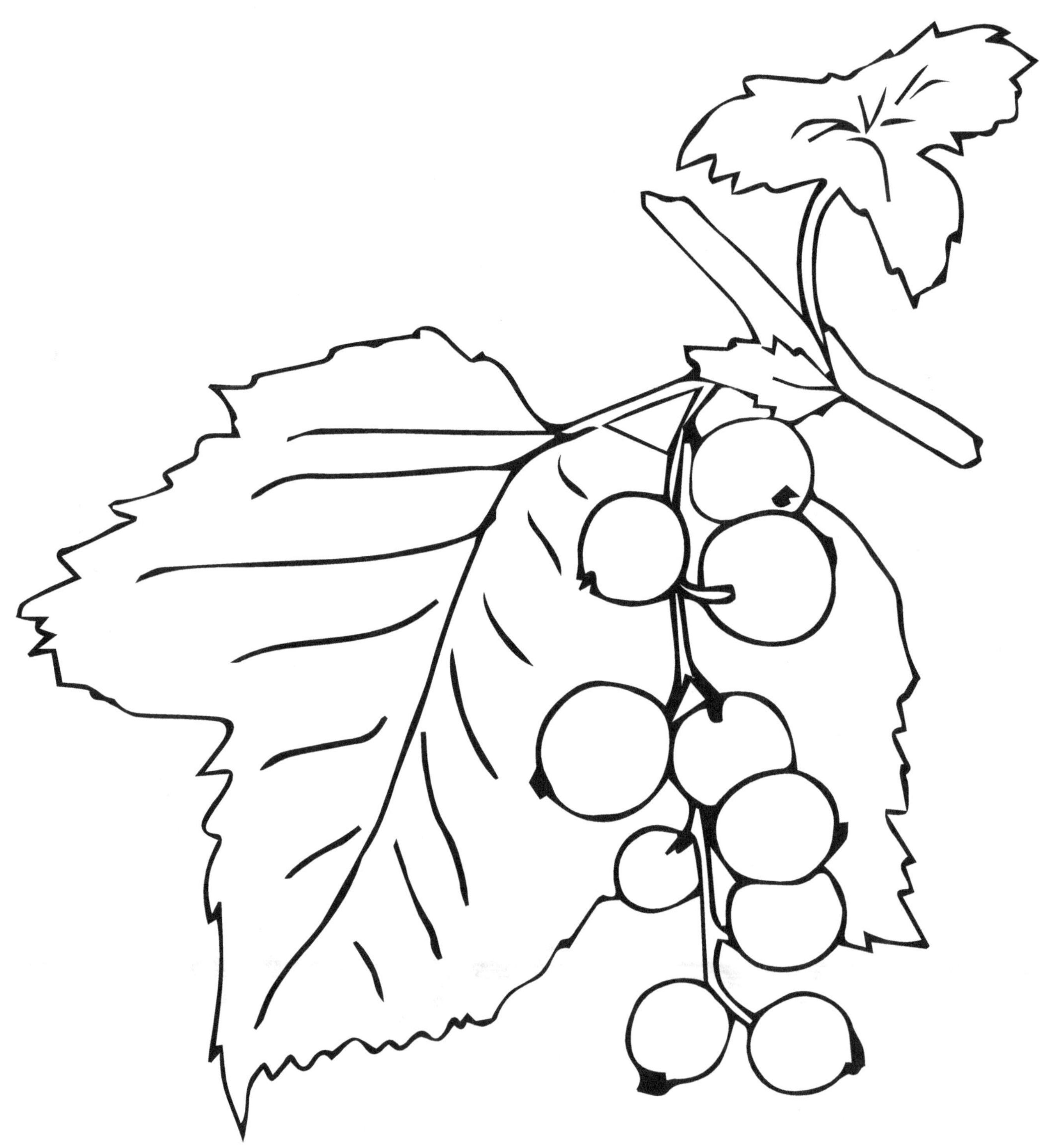

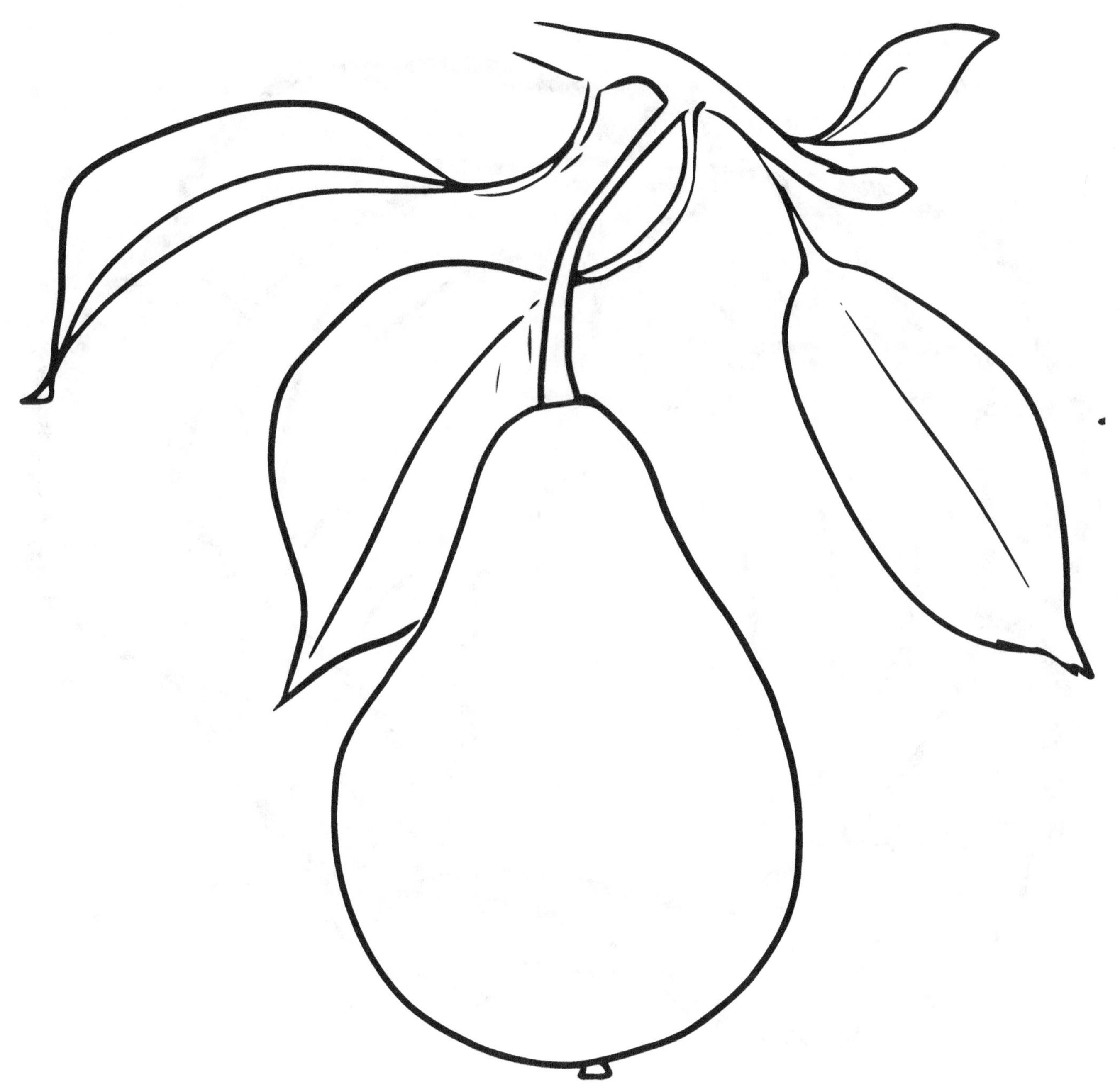

www.FoodHero.org

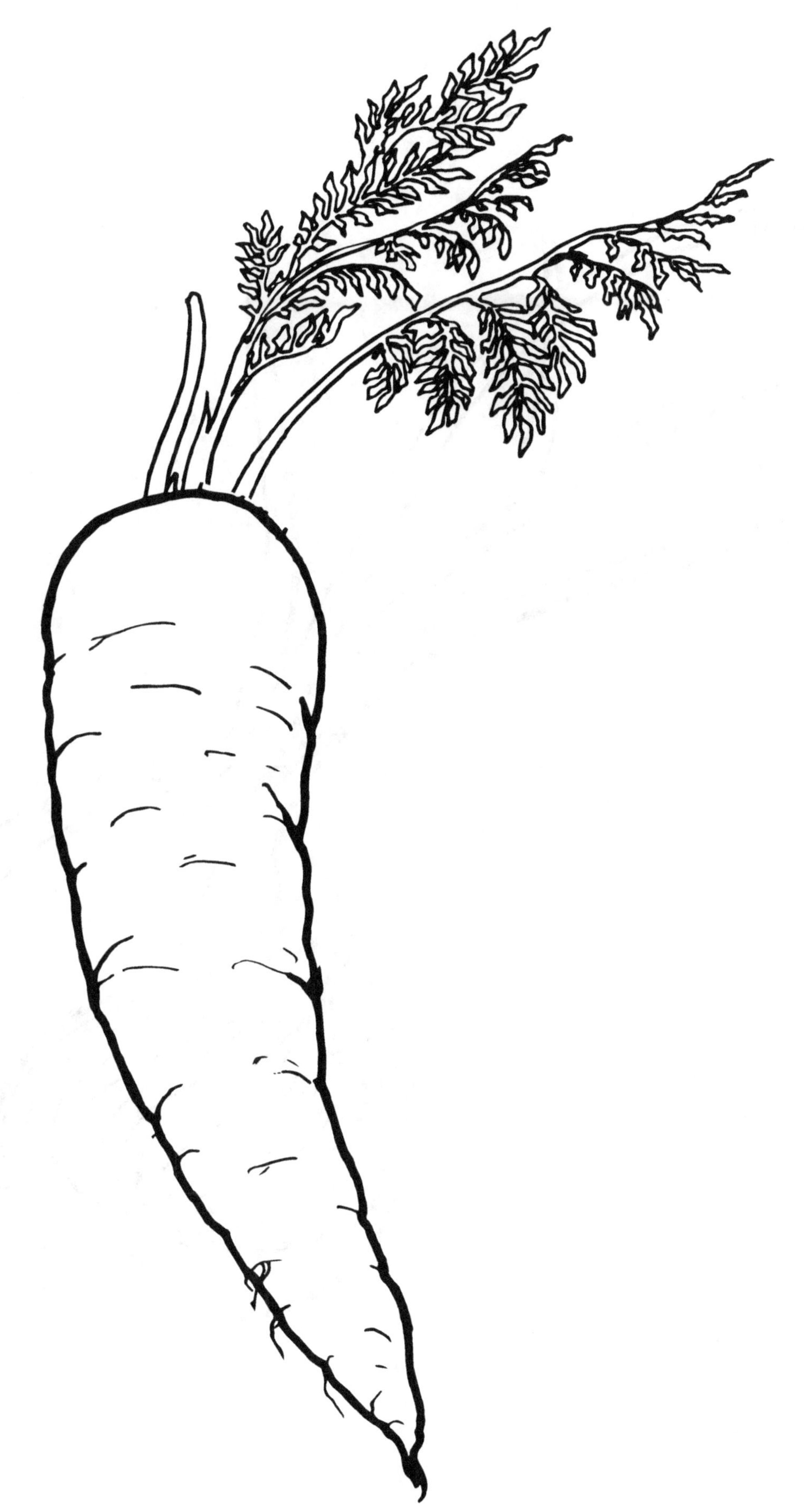

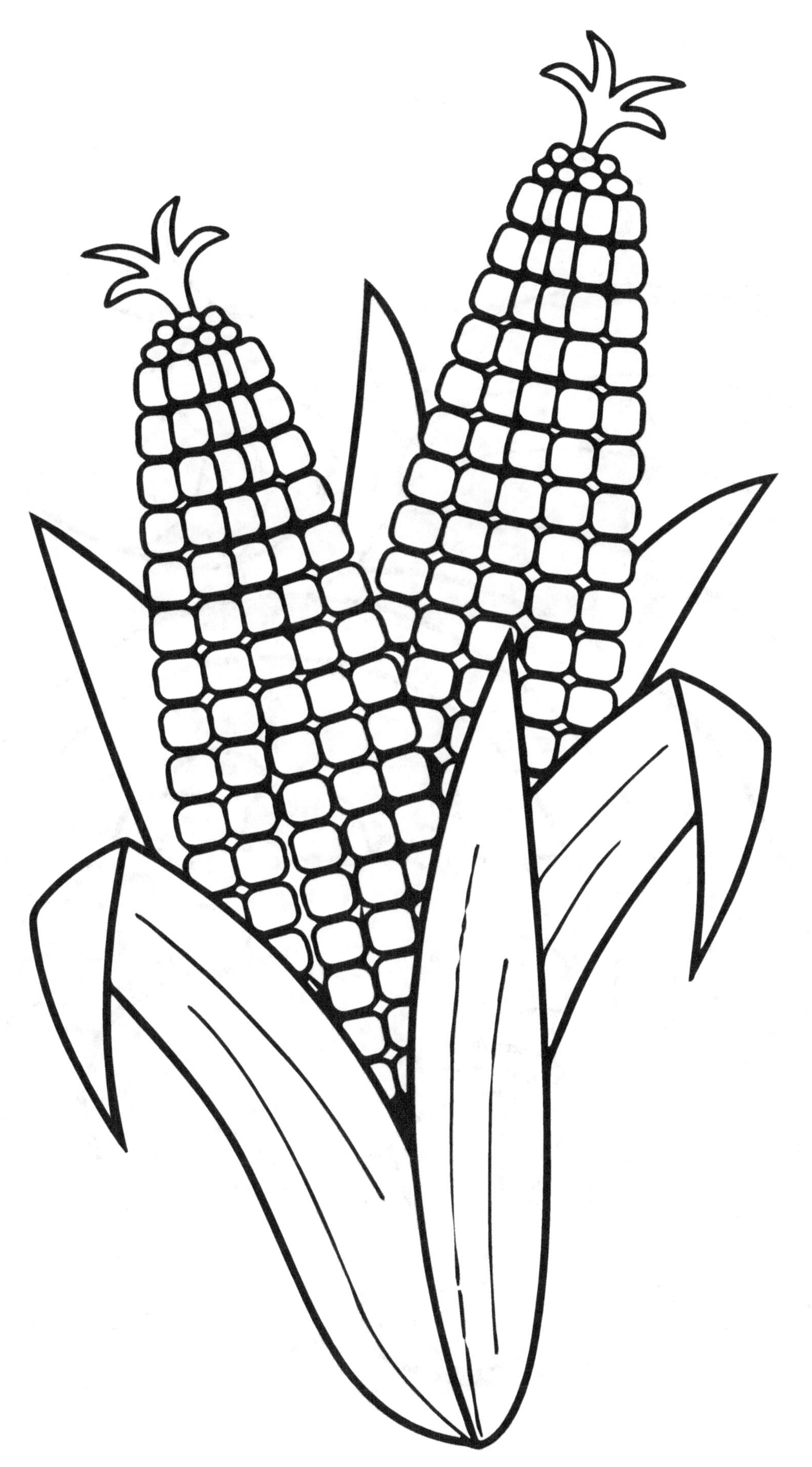

no.2
no. 2
16

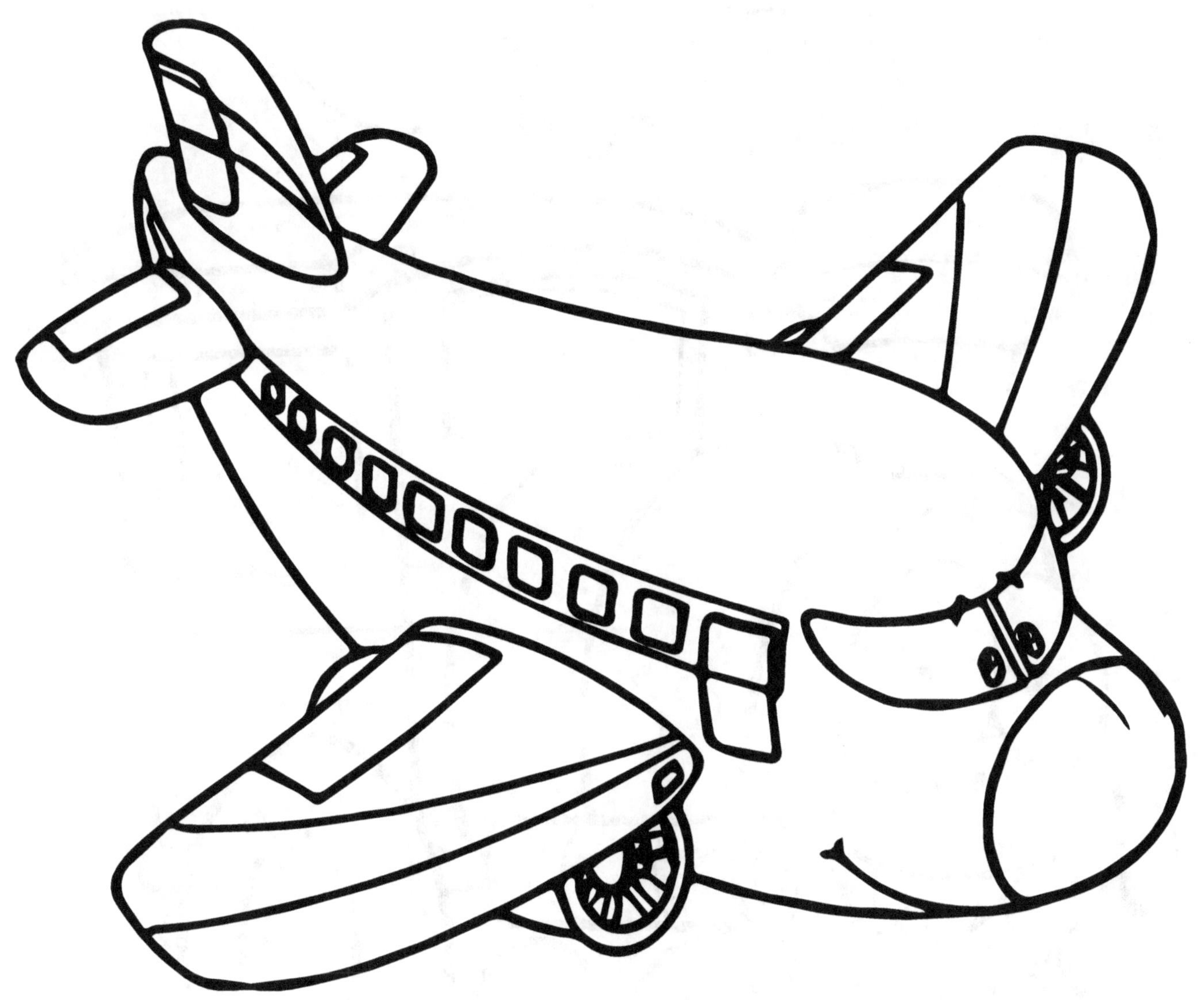

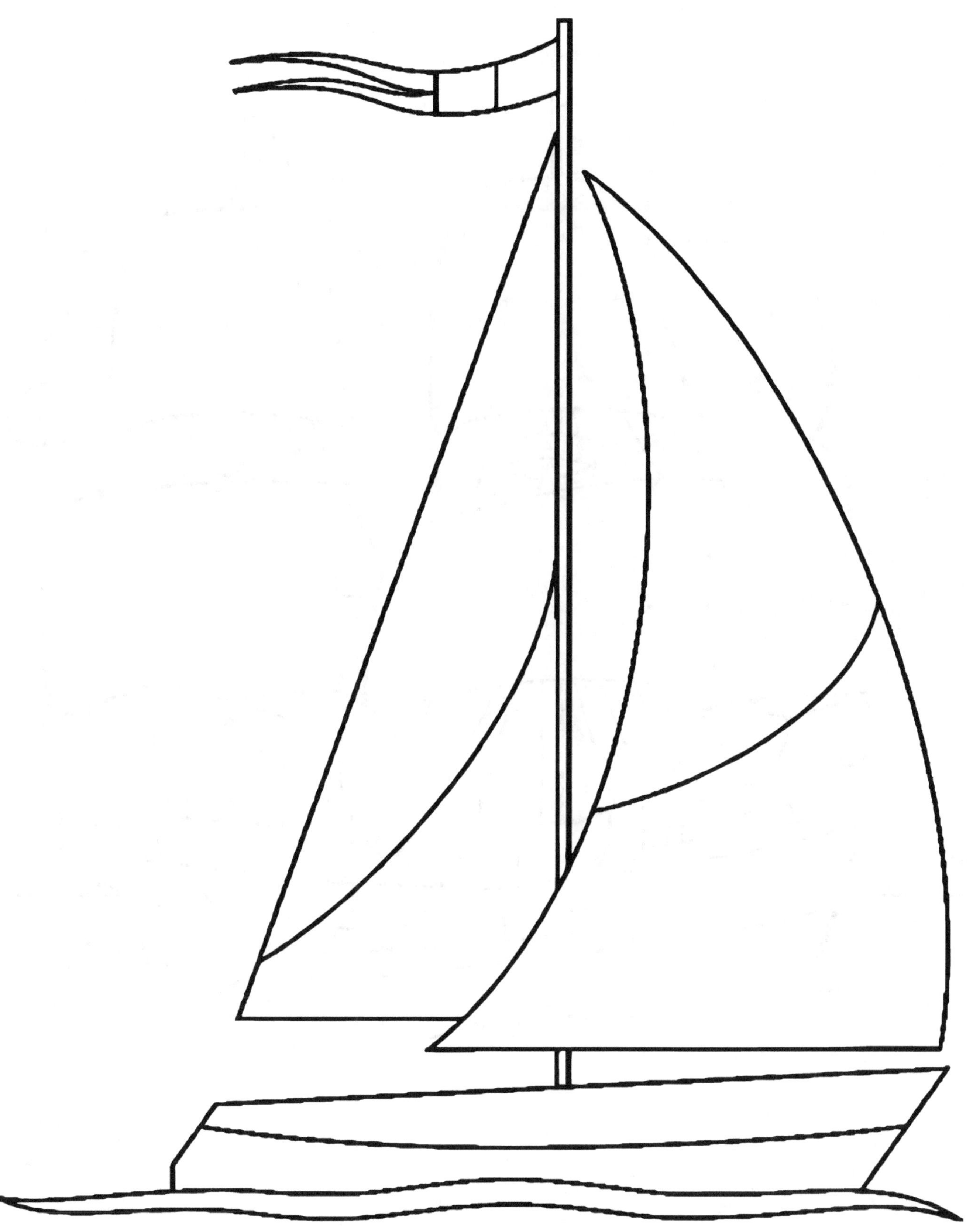

www.ingramcontent.com/pod-product-compliance
Lightning Source LLC
Chambersburg PA
CBHW081728250726
48657CB00010B/3174